JED RAMOS

ChatGPT for Linguists

Revolutionize Language Research and
Analysis with AI-Driven Insights
(2024 Guide)

Copyright © 2024 by Jed Ramos

All rights reserved. No part of this publication may be reproduced, stored or transmitted in any form or by any means, electronic, mechanical, photocopying, recording, scanning, or otherwise without written permission from the publisher. It is illegal to copy this book, post it to a website, or distribute it by any other means without permission.

First edition

This book was professionally typeset on Reedsy.
Find out more at reedsy.com

Contents

1. Introduction to ChatGPT for Linguists — 1
2. Utilizing ChatGPT for Language Tasks — 4
3. Interpretation with ChatGPT — 7
4. Utilizing ChatGPT for Language Acquisition — 9
5. Utilizing ChatGPT for Enhancing Pronunciation and Accent — 12
6. Utilizing ChatGPT for Language Instruction and Evaluation — 15
7. The realm of multilingual chatbots and customer service — 18
8. Utilizing ChatGPT for Linguistic Investigation — 21
9. Addressing Ethical Concerns in AI-Facilitated Linguistic... — 25
10. Anticipating the Future: ChatGPT and the Evolution of... — 28

1

Introduction to ChatGPT for Linguists

I'm an AI language model, and I'm here to give linguists an introduction to ChatGPT. ChatGPT, developed by OpenAI, is a sophisticated deep learning language model capable of producing text across various styles and formats, including news articles, essays, and social media posts. Linguists can leverage ChatGPT to delve into language patterns and create natural language text for diverse research and practical purposes.

Trained on an extensive dataset comprising internet text like books, articles, and more, ChatGPT employs deep learning methods to grasp statistical patterns and connections between words and sentences. It then generates text resembling the input data.

For linguists, ChatGPT offers myriad applications, including analyzing language patterns, producing new language data for research, and crafting language models for various language processing tasks. With its adeptness in generating coherent and natural text, ChatGPT holds promise in revolutionizing the realms of linguistics and language processing.

Some envisioned applications of ChatGPT in linguistics encompass:

- Language analysis: Delving into language patterns and investigating

word and syntax relationships.
- Language modeling: Generating language models for tasks like language translation, sentiment analysis, and speech recognition.
- Language generation: Creating fresh language data for research, especially beneficial for languages with scarce linguistic resources.
- Language teaching: Crafting language exercises and quizzes for learners, as well as developing interactive language learning tools.

Overall, ChatGPT emerges as a potent instrument for linguists, offering numerous avenues for language research, analysis, and processing. With ongoing technological advancements, we anticipate witnessing further innovative applications of ChatGPT in the linguistic domain.

Understanding ChatGPT

ChatGPT, an extensive artificial intelligence language model, was created by OpenAI. It operates on the architecture of Generative Pre-trained Transformer 3.5 (GPT-3.5), aimed at generating natural language text. ChatGPT exhibits versatility in various language tasks such as translation, question-answering, and summarization. It undergoes training with a vast amount of textual data and utilizes deep learning techniques to produce text that closely resembles human-written content. This innovation holds the potential to transform numerous domains within linguistics, including natural language processing, machine translation, and text analysis.

The Role of AI in Linguistics

In the field of linguistics, artificial intelligence serves to process extensive language datasets to discern patterns, categorize languages, and construct models for language acquisition and usage. Additionally, AI aids in language translation, teaching, and speech recognition.

A notable advantage of AI in linguistics lies in its capacity to swiftly and accurately handle large volumes of data. This capability facilitates linguists in recognizing linguistic patterns and correlations across different language facets, thereby enabling the development of more nuanced models regarding language acquisition and usage. Moreover, AI streamlines many traditionally manual tasks undertaken by linguists, such as transcription and annotation, thereby saving time and minimizing errors, allowing linguists to delve into more intricate endeavors.

Another domain witnessing AI's impact in linguistics is the enhancement of language translation tools. These tools employ machine learning algorithms to analyze vast language datasets, thereby identifying patterns and relationships among different languages. This process contributes to enhancing the precision and efficiency of language translation while expanding its accessibility to a broader audience.

Overall, AI is instrumental in expanding our understanding of language and its mechanisms, while simultaneously making language learning and translation more accessible on a global scale.

2

Utilizing ChatGPT for Language Tasks

ChatGPT offers a versatile solution for language tasks, including translation endeavors within linguistics. Leveraging its capacity to comprehend natural language and produce responses akin to humans, it can deliver translations that surpass the accuracy and naturalness of conventional machine translation techniques. Moreover, ChatGPT facilitates real-time translation, enabling the interpretation of live conversations and occurrences in multiple languages. This feature proves invaluable for international conferences, meetings, and diverse events involving participants conversing in different languages.

Additionally, ChatGPT aids linguists in crafting multilingual resources such as dictionaries and terminology lists. Through training, it discerns patterns and correlations among words and phrases across various languages, simplifying the creation of precise and extensive language references. Overall, ChatGPT harbors the potential to transform the landscape of linguistics, expediting translation and language processing while enhancing accuracy and accessibility.

Leveraging AI Assistance for Text Translation

Harnessing ChatGPT as a tool for text translation can yield efficient outcomes. Trained on extensive parallel texts in diverse languages, the model acquires the capability to generate precise translations. The quality of translations hinges on the caliber and quantity of training data and the complexity of the text under translation.

To initiate translation with ChatGPT, input the text in the source language and employ the model to produce the corresponding text in the target language. Human intervention can further refine the output to ensure accuracy and fluency. The swiftness of AI translation proves advantageous in scenarios necessitating rapid processing of voluminous text, such as news reporting or business document translation. However, it is essential to acknowledge that AI translation may not always be flawless, necessitating human oversight to uphold precision.

In essence, ChatGPT emerges as a potent asset for language professionals seeking to streamline translation workflows and bolster efficiency.

Leveraging ChatGPT for Localization Efforts

ChatGPT's utility extends to localization endeavors through training on substantial volumes of text data in the target language. This approach empowers the AI model to generate text that resonates as natural and authentic in the target language.

To employ ChatGPT for localization, furnish it with a copious corpus of text in the target language, encompassing news articles, social media content, or website materials. Fine-tuning the model on this data via transfer learning enables adaptation to the new task or domain.

Once refined, the model produces text in the target language that surpasses the authenticity of non-native speaker output. This capability proves advantageous for businesses and organizations aiming to engage a global audience by crafting localized content tailored to their target market's preferences.

Beyond text translation, ChatGPT supports speech recognition and synthesis, further enhancing the localization process. By incorporating audio data in the target language, the model can be trained to recognize and generate speech with heightened naturalness and fluency.

3

Interpretation with ChatGPT

Interpretation involves converting spoken language from one language to another. This can occur either consecutively, where the interpreter listens to the speaker and then translates into the target language, or simultaneously, where the interpreter translates in real-time as the speaker talks.

Utilizing ChatGPT can assist in interpretation by offering real-time translation during conversations, which proves beneficial in scenarios with language barriers, like international business meetings or conferences. The interpreter can swiftly translate the speech using ChatGPT and convey it to the audience in the desired language.

Moreover, ChatGPT can transcribe speech into text, aiding in situations requiring content analysis, such as legal or medical contexts.

Improving Interpretation with AI

AI can enhance interpretation by providing real-time translation, transcribing speech, and generating summaries. ChatGPT serves as a tool for quick translations and summaries, aiding interpreters. It can also transcribe audio or video files into text, facilitating linguists in managing large datasets. Furthermore, ChatGPT can assist in identifying language nuances like slang and regional dialects, ensuring accurate and culturally appropriate interpretation. Additionally, it offers suggestions for terminology or phrasing, enhancing interpretation quality and consistency.

Real-time Interpretation with ChatGPT

Real-time interpretation with ChatGPT involves using its natural language processing capabilities to instantly translate spoken language during conversations. This proves useful in scenarios where individuals speaking different languages need to communicate, such as in international business meetings or medical consultations.

The process entails using speech recognition software to transcribe spoken language into text, followed by ChatGPT's language model capabilities to translate the text. The translated text is then converted into speech using text-to-speech technology.

While ChatGPT can handle complex sentences and idiomatic expressions common in everyday language, it's important to acknowledge that current AI models may contain translation errors. Therefore, ChatGPT should be utilized as a tool to aid interpretation rather than replacing human interpreters.

4

Utilizing ChatGPT for Language Acquisition

The realm of language acquisition stands poised for a transformation through the integration of AI and machine learning technologies. ChatGPT emerges as a valuable asset in this evolution, capable of generating conversational exchanges across various languages and delivering immediate feedback to learners. Here's how ChatGPT can be leveraged for language learning:

1. Conversational Proficiency: ChatGPT facilitates conversational practice in diverse languages, enabling learners to hone their speaking and listening skills in an authentic and stimulating manner. This feature proves especially beneficial for individuals lacking access to native speakers or unable to immerse themselves in environments where their desired language is spoken.
2. Writing Enhancement: Additionally, ChatGPT aids learners in refining their writing skills in the target language by generating prompts and furnishing feedback on grammar, vocabulary usage, and syntax.
3. Vocabulary Enrichment: ChatGPT serves as a resource for constructing vocabulary banks, offering elucidations and contextual examples for

word usage. Moreover, it suggests synonyms and antonyms to assist learners in broadening their lexicon.
4. Cultural Insight: ChatGPT furnishes learners with cultural context, illuminating linguistic usage across various cultures. It generates responses infused with cultural references and elucidates customs and practices unique to different societies.
5. Accent Refinement: ChatGPT aids learners in mitigating their accents in the target language by providing responses and feedback on pronunciation, intonation, and stress patterns.
6. Tailored Learning: ChatGPT personalizes language learning experiences by crafting content aligned with learners' interests and learning preferences, while also adapting to their progress and requirements.

In essence, ChatGPT stands poised to revolutionize the language learning landscape. By delivering instantaneous feedback and generating captivating content, it has the potential to streamline and enrich the language acquisition journey, rendering it both efficient and enjoyable.

Enhancing Language Skills with AI

Utilizing ChatGPT for language learning can be highly beneficial. One approach involves presenting users with prompts and exercises to reinforce vocabulary and grammar. These exercises might entail completing sentences with the appropriate words or phrases, translating between languages, or vice versa. Furthermore, ChatGPT can offer feedback on users' responses, pinpointing grammatical errors and suggesting corrections, while also providing explanations and examples to aid comprehension.

Moreover, ChatGPT customizes the learning experience by adapting to each user's proficiency level and preferred learning style. It tailors the difficulty of exercises based on performance and offers supplementary resources and tips to address specific challenges. Additionally, ChatGPT facilitates immersive learning by engaging users in simulated conversations in the target language, fostering natural development of listening and speaking skills.

Developing Linguistic Proficiency with ChatGPT

Certainly, ChatGPT plays a pivotal role in fostering language proficiency by generating writing prompts, offering feedback on exercises, and addressing language-related queries. Its ability to simulate conversations in the target language is particularly valuable for enhancing speaking and listening capabilities. Moreover, the feature of real-time translation of spoken language serves as a practical tool for honing speaking and listening skills in a foreign language.

However, it's imperative to recognize that ChatGPT should complement traditional language learning methods rather than serve as a sole resource. Human interaction and feedback remain indispensable components of language acquisition, and ChatGPT cannot fully replicate these aspects.

5

Utilizing ChatGPT for Enhancing Pronunciation and Accent

ChatGPT offers a valuable resource for individuals seeking to refine their pronunciation and accent. It possesses the capability to evaluate oral communication, offering insights into pronunciation accuracy and intonation. This feature proves particularly advantageous for language learners striving to enhance their verbal abilities and achieve a more authentic fluency in their target language.

Leveraging sophisticated machine learning algorithms, ChatGPT can detect recurring patterns and typical pronunciation errors, delivering tailored feedback to aid improvement. Moreover, it can generate tailored exercises and drills to facilitate learners' practice in honing their pronunciation and intonation.

Moreover, ChatGPT serves as a tool for honing conversational skills and bolstering fluency. Through analysis of both written and spoken language, it identifies commonly used phrases and expressions, offering guidance on their appropriate contextual usage. This functionality is especially beneficial for learners aiming to imbue their speech with a natural and confident demeanor.

In conclusion, ChatGPT stands as an invaluable asset for language learners endeavoring to refine their pronunciation, accent, and conversational proficiency.

Utilizing AI for Pronunciation and Accent Enhancement

Employing ChatGPT for refining pronunciation and accent involves providing learners with immediate feedback and correction. For instance, an AI-driven speech recognition system could assess a learner's pronunciation and accent, offering real-time suggestions for improvement. This proves particularly beneficial for language learners lacking access to native speakers for feedback. AI-based pronunciation tools further offer personalized feedback and tailored practice exercises to cater to individual learner requirements. By analyzing a learner's speech patterns, these tools identify areas needing improvement and offer targeted exercises to address them. Moreover, ChatGPT serves as a platform for learners to practice pronunciation and accent within realistic contexts. For example, interacting with a ChatGPT-powered virtual assistant enables learners to hone their conversational skills and receive feedback on pronunciation and accent, thereby enhancing their ability to communicate effectively in real-world scenarios.

Enhancing Listening Comprehension with ChatGPT

ChatGPT also facilitates the development of listening comprehension skills among language learners. Through its capability to generate spoken responses, ChatGPT aids in practicing listening and responding in a foreign language. Users can input spoken sentences or phrases in the target language, and ChatGPT generates spoken responses for them to listen to and comprehend. Additionally, ChatGPT can produce audio recordings of texts in the target language, enabling learners to practice comprehension of various accents and dialects.

6

Utilizing ChatGPT for Language Instruction and Evaluation

ChatGPT emerges as a valuable asset for both language teaching and assessment endeavors. Leveraging its text generation capabilities alongside interactive features, it fosters an environment conducive to natural language conversations, thereby facilitating language learning and evaluation.

Various applications underscore ChatGPT's utility in language pedagogy and assessment:

1. Exercise Generation: Language educators harness ChatGPT to craft exercises for students. By furnishing prompts and soliciting responses, instructors can utilize ChatGPT to generate sample answers, enabling students to dissect and assess them.
2. Feedback Provision: ChatGPT assumes a role in furnishing feedback to language learners. Students can submit their written work, and ChatGPT can analyze it, offering insights on grammar, vocabulary employment, and other linguistic facets.
3. Conversational Drill: Learners engage in conversational practice facilitated by ChatGPT. Interacting in a natural language discourse aids in

honing speaking and listening proficiencies.
4. Language Evaluation: ChatGPT serves as a means for evaluating language skills. It can assess listening comprehension by playing audio snippets followed by relevant queries. Similarly, it gauges reading comprehension through text-based passages accompanied by associated questions.

In essence, ChatGPT emerges as a valuable adjunct for language education and evaluation endeavors. It not only affords learners the opportunity to hone their language competencies within an interactive milieu but also empowers instructors to devise tailored exercises and appraise language proficiencies effectively.

Tailored Learning Plans Enhanced by AI

ChatGPT excels in crafting personalized learning plans tailored to individual learners' needs. By examining various data points such as a learner's performance, interests, and preferred learning methods, ChatGPT can generate bespoke lessons and exercises. Moreover, it can oversee progress, acknowledge achievements, and offer guidance on areas requiring enhancement.

For instance, ChatGPT can formulate quizzes and interactive activities that adjust to the learner's skill level and pace. It also has the capacity to produce study materials like flashcards, summaries, and visual aids tailored to the learner's preferred style. Furthermore, ChatGPT continuously monitors the learner's advancement and modifies the learning plan as needed to ensure optimal outcomes.

Language Evaluation and Testing with ChatGPT

Evaluating language proficiency is crucial in language education, and ChatGPT plays a valuable role in this domain by offering language assessment tools driven by natural language processing (NLP) and machine learning algorithms.

ChatGPT evaluates language proficiency levels by analyzing written and spoken language samples. This assessment includes identifying grammatical errors, gauging vocabulary breadth, assessing pronunciation and intonation, and evaluating reading and listening comprehension skills. Additionally, ChatGPT crafts tailored language learning plans based on individual learner requirements and objectives, integrating personalized exercises and materials to address weaknesses and reinforce strengths.

Moreover, ChatGPT facilitates language learning and teaching through interactive chatbots and language tutors. These resources provide personalized feedback, conversational practice, and simulations of real-life language scenarios to bolster communication abilities.

To sum up, ChatGPT enhances language assessment and testing by delivering precise and customized proficiency evaluations. It also supports language education by offering interactive chatbots and language tutors to refine communication skills.

7

The realm of multilingual chatbots and customer service

The realm of multilingual chatbots and customer service is expanding, presenting a significant opportunity for ChatGPT's involvement. These chatbots can be programmed to interact with customers and offer assistance in various languages. Leveraging ChatGPT, these chatbots can exhibit advanced language skills and deliver responses that feel more natural compared to conventional ones.

To illustrate, a chatbot could be configured to address common customer inquiries across multiple languages, furnish product details, or facilitate transactions in a language preferred by the customer. Such capabilities empower companies to deliver superior customer service and support, especially benefiting multilingual customers who might struggle with languages they aren't proficient in.

Moreover, chatbots contribute to cost reduction for companies by automating repetitive tasks and diminishing the necessity for human customer service representatives. This, in turn, allows human agents to concentrate on more intricate tasks and offer tailored assistance to customers.

Nonetheless, it's crucial to recognize that while ChatGPT-powered chatbots excel at handling routine tasks and addressing common queries, they may lack the ability to tackle complex issues or offer the same level of empathy and personal connection as human agents. Striking a balance between automation and human interaction is key to delivering the optimal customer service experience.

Creating Multilingual Chatbots with ChatGPT

ChatGPT offers the capability to create multilingual chatbots, which are computer programs designed to mimic human conversation and serve various purposes such as customer support, marketing, and information provision. Thanks to advancements in AI, chatbots have evolved to understand natural language and engage in more conversational interactions.

Utilizing ChatGPT, developers can train chatbots in multiple languages, enabling them to interact with users in different linguistic backgrounds. This feature proves especially beneficial for businesses operating internationally or catering to diverse language-speaking clientele. By delivering services or information in users' preferred languages, multilingual chatbots enhance user experience and foster higher customer satisfaction.

Moreover, integrating chatbots with machine translation services facilitates real-time language translation for users who don't speak the chatbot's language. This integration broadens the chatbot's utility and accessibility, reaching a more extensive audience.

Nevertheless, creating a multilingual chatbot necessitates thorough planning, considering language subtleties, cultural disparities, and potential biases. Ensuring the chatbot remains culturally sensitive and delivers accurate and helpful information across all supported languages is paramount.

Enhancing Customer Service through Artificial Intelligence

Artificial intelligence (AI) holds the potential to enhance customer service significantly by offering prompt and tailored replies to customers' inquiries and issues. Utilizing AI, chatbots can manage routine customer questions, such as inquiries about products, pricing, and order status, thereby allowing human agents to focus on more intricate matters. Furthermore, chatbots can deliver round-the-clock customer assistance, enhancing accessibility and responsiveness.

These chatbots can be programmed to converse in various languages, making them beneficial for businesses catering to a global clientele. Through the application of machine learning, chatbots can also refine their responses by learning from past interactions, thereby elevating the overall customer experience.

Moreover, AI-powered sentiment analysis can be employed to monitor and analyze customer feedback across social media platforms and other channels, enabling companies to promptly identify and address concerns. This proactive approach fosters customer trust and loyalty, ultimately contributing to increased revenue and business growth.

8

Utilizing ChatGPT for Linguistic Investigation

ChatGPT offers a versatile toolset for linguistic inquiry across various domains. A prominent application lies in its contribution to the advancement of natural language processing (NLP) and natural language understanding (NLU) technologies. These advancements empower computers to effectively process, scrutinize, and comprehend human language, thereby finding utility in diverse fields like machine translation, sentiment analysis, and conversational AI.

Moreover, ChatGPT serves as a valuable asset in linguistic research by facilitating the generation of text in multiple languages, thereby aiding tasks such as corpus development, machine translation, and language modeling. Additionally, its capacity to analyze extensive textual data allows for the identification of underlying patterns or trends, proving beneficial in computational linguistics, sociolinguistics, and discourse analysis.

Furthermore, ChatGPT's capabilities extend to the creation of chatbots that mimic human conversation, serving as aids in language learning or practice. Lastly, it contributes to sentiment analysis by discerning the emotional tone and sentiment conveyed within text, offering insights applicable to fields like marketing and public opinion research.

Utilizing Artificial Intelligence for Linguistic Research and Examination

Artificial intelligence (AI) proves advantageous in linguistic research and analysis through various avenues. Here are several illustrations:

1. Natural Language Processing (NLP): NLP, a domain within AI, focuses on the interaction between computers and human languages. Leveraging NLP techniques, linguists can delve into extensive text datasets, recognizing patterns and deriving insightful conclusions. For instance, NLP aids in scrutinizing the syntax, semantics, and pragmatics of languages, alongside identifying linguistic aspects like tone, sentiment, and register.
2. Corpus Linguistics: This methodology employs vast text collections, known as corpora, to explore language intricacies. With AI tools, linguists can swiftly construct and analyze corpora. They utilize machine learning algorithms to categorize and annotate texts automatically, uncovering usage patterns in specific languages.
3. Speech Recognition and Synthesis: AI facilitates the examination and generation of spoken language. Linguists employ speech recognition algorithms to transcribe oral communication into written form, thereby scrutinizing phonetics and phonology. Additionally, text-to-speech synthesis aids in generating authentic verbal output in various languages.
4. Language Revitalization: AI contributes to the preservation of endangered languages. Through machine learning algorithms, linguists can automate transcription and translation of spoken language. Moreover, AI assists in crafting language learning aids and materials.

In essence, AI serves as a valuable asset for linguists across diverse research domains. However, it's imperative to employ AI ethically and conscientiously, acknowledging potential biases and constraints within AI models.

Utilizing ChatGPT for Linguistic Data Mining

The process of linguistic data mining entails scrutinizing extensive language datasets to uncover trends and insights, enhancing our comprehension of language and its application across various scenarios. ChatGPT serves as a valuable tool for such endeavors, facilitating tasks like text classification, sentiment analysis, topic modeling, and named entity recognition.

Text classification involves sorting texts into predefined categories, such as positive, negative, or neutral sentiments, for instance, classifying tweets based on their emotional content. ChatGPT can undergo training on substantial text datasets, enabling it to classify new texts according to their contents.

Sentiment analysis, a subset of text classification, endeavors to discern the emotional tenor of textual content, often applied in assessing customer feedback on social media or gauging sentiment in news articles. ChatGPT can be trained to detect positive, negative, and neutral sentiments within text data.

Topic modeling, another method, identifies prevalent themes or subjects within vast collections of texts by scrutinizing word co-occurrences and grouping them based on similarities. ChatGPT proves adept at generating topic models from extensive text datasets, facilitating the comprehension of core themes and issues within the corpus.

Named entity recognition involves pinpointing and extracting specific entities like individuals, organizations, or locations from textual data.

ChatGPT can be trained to identify such entities within texts, allowing for analysis of their distribution and frequency across different contexts.

Overall, ChatGPT stands as a potent instrument for linguists seeking to analyze and comprehend extensive language datasets. By streamlining many laborious and time-consuming tasks inherent in linguistic data mining, ChatGPT empowers researchers to uncover fresh insights and patterns in language utilization more efficiently and effectively.

9

Addressing Ethical Concerns in AI-Facilitated Linguistic Endeavors

When employing ChatGPT for linguistic purposes, ethical dimensions necessitate careful consideration, akin to any utilization of AI. Several pivotal factors merit attention:

1. Bias: AI frameworks may perpetuate or intensify biases ingrained in their training data. Vigilance regarding biases within the data and efforts to alleviate them are crucial when utilizing ChatGPT for linguistics.
2. Privacy: ChatGPT relies on extensive datasets, some of which may contain sensitive information. Ethical acquisition and utilization of data for training and testing are imperative.
3. Transparency: Deciphering the rationale behind AI-generated outcomes, such as those from ChatGPT, can pose challenges. Ensuring transparency and comprehensibility in AI applications is paramount.
4. Responsibility: ChatGPT and similar AI systems serve as tools, placing the onus on human users to ensure ethical and responsible usage.
5. Human involvement: Incorporating human oversight and intervention remains essential when employing AI in linguistic endeavors. While ChatGPT offers substantial capabilities, human judgment and expertise

remain irreplaceable.
6. Fairness: Upholding fairness in linguistic applications of ChatGPT involves preventing discrimination against individuals or groups, including considerations such as language and cultural biases, as well as biases related to accents or dialects.

By addressing these ethical considerations and others, it becomes feasible to utilize ChatGPT for linguistics in a responsible and advantageous manner.

Discussing Bias and Ethics in AI Language Tools

When employing artificial intelligence in linguistic tasks, ethical considerations are paramount. One significant concern revolves around bias, which can manifest in language models due to the biases inherent in the training data. For instance, if a language model is trained on texts predominantly authored by white males, it might struggle when confronted with texts from diverse backgrounds.

To mitigate bias, it's crucial to utilize varied and inclusive datasets during model training. Moreover, continuous testing and evaluation are necessary to detect and rectify any biases or inaccuracies.

Transparency is another key aspect. The inner workings of language models can be opaque, posing challenges in identifying and addressing biases or errors. To tackle this, researchers are exploring ways to develop AI models that are more transparent and explainable.

Additionally, accountability is essential. As AI language tools advance, there's a risk they might be misused to generate misleading or harmful content. Therefore, implementing systems to ensure responsible usage and address any negative impacts is vital.

Ensuring Privacy and Security in Linguistic Data

Preserving privacy and security in linguistic data is indispensable for the ethical application of AI in linguistics. Linguistic data often contains personal information, necessitating strict confidentiality measures to safeguard individuals' privacy.

To uphold privacy and security, employing secure data storage methods and encryption protocols is crucial. Access to linguistic data should be tightly regulated, granting authorization only to personnel authorized to handle sensitive information.

Moreover, obtaining informed consent from individuals before utilizing their linguistic data for research or analysis is paramount. This entails providing individuals with comprehensive information regarding data usage, access permissions, and privacy safeguards.

Finally, transparency regarding the use of AI in linguistics is essential. This includes elucidating the processes of data collection, processing, and utilization, fostering trust with the public and ensuring individuals are informed about the handling of their linguistic data.

10

Anticipating the Future: ChatGPT and the Evolution of Linguistics

As advancements in artificial intelligence (AI) and natural language processing (NLP) persist, the trajectory of linguistics appears poised to undergo substantial transformation under their influence. Notably, tools like ChatGPT and similar language models are demonstrating their prowess across various domains, including language translation, interpretation, language acquisition, and linguistic exploration.

Looking ahead, it's foreseeable that AI will become even more deeply intertwined with our daily lives, facilitating enhanced cross-lingual communication and dismantling age-old barriers to interaction. Additionally, AI holds promise in bolstering researchers' comprehension of linguistic mechanisms and their contextual usage.

Nevertheless, the integration of AI into linguistic realms raises pertinent ethical and societal concerns. It's imperative to ensure the development and utilization of AI language tools adhere to principles of fairness, impartiality, and utmost regard for individual privacy and security. As AI permeates further into our societal fabric, collaborative efforts among linguists, AI developers, policymakers, and relevant stakeholders will be indispensable in navigating these ethical complexities and ensuring equitable distribution of AI benefits.

Current Patterns and Future Projections

Recent strides in AI-facilitated linguistics encompass the refinement of sophisticated NLP algorithms, harnessing machine learning for language modeling, and the expanding domain of AI in speech recognition and synthesis. These advancements have markedly enhanced automated translation, interpretation, and language learning, among other functionalities.

Looking forward, AI's role in linguistics is poised to amplify, with continued enhancements in NLP, speech recognition, and language modeling. Furthermore, AI may drive the development of more advanced language learning tools, featuring personalized learning trajectories and virtual tutoring.

A burgeoning trend lies in the burgeoning application of AI within computational linguistics, entailing the examination of natural languages' computational facets. This avenue of inquiry could pave the way for novel AI applications in domains such as machine translation, text-to-speech synthesis, and speech recognition.

In summation, it's evident that AI will wield considerable influence over the landscape of linguistics in the foreseeable future, spanning both research endeavors and practical implementations. However, it's imperative that these advancements proceed with ethical underpinnings, encompassing the preservation of linguistic data privacy and security, alongside the mitigation of bias and the pursuit of fairness in AI language utilities.

Embracing Artificial Intelligence in Language Studies

CHATGPT FOR LINGUISTS: TRANSLATION, INTERPRETATION AND LANGUAGE LEARNING

Similar to various other domains, AI is already exerting its influence within the realm of language studies, with this impact expected to persist in the years to come. Current trends and forthcoming predictions encompass:

1. Enhanced Language Acquisition: AI-driven language learning tools are advancing, providing learners with personalized feedback and customized lesson plans. With ongoing AI enhancements, language acquisition is poised to become even more streamlined and impactful.

2. Improved Translation and Interpretation: AI is presently enhancing translation and interpretation capabilities, a trajectory likely to continue. The future may witness broader adoption of real-time interpretation tools utilizing AI for more precise and efficient translation services.

3. Proliferation of Multilingual Chatbots: In response to businesses' needs to engage with diverse clientele, the development of multilingual chatbots is anticipated. Advancements in natural language processing and machine learning will likely facilitate this evolution.

4. Heightened Linguistic Research: AI is currently aiding linguists in analyzing extensive datasets and uncovering intricate patterns often elusive via traditional research methods. This synergy between AI and linguistic research is poised to persist and expand as AI sophistication increases.

5. Amplified Ethical Considerations: As with any AI application, ethical contemplation is crucial when employing AI-driven linguistic tools. Addressing biases, ensuring fairness and privacy, and promoting responsible, ethical use of linguistic data are imperative facets of this discourse.

In summary, AI is poised to assume a progressively significant role in language studies, fostering more effective cross-cultural communication and deeper comprehension of linguistic intricacies.

www.ingramcontent.com/pod-product-compliance
Lightning Source LLC
LaVergne TN
LVHW021050100526
838202LV00082B/5416